D0267082

Common Cause for Nature

A practical guide to values
and frames in conservation

This report was produced with the support and input of the following partner organisations. The authors are grateful to staff in these partner organisations for their openness in reflecting on what they have learned from the research that they commissioned, and in reflecting on the implications that they foresee for their organisations. However, the specific recommendations of this report were developed by PIRC, and are their sole responsibility.

Bat Conservation Trust, Buglife, Campaign to Protect Rural England, John Muir Award, The Mammal Society, Marine Conservation Society, The Ramblers, Royal Society for the Protection of Birds, The Wildlife Trusts, The Conservation Volunteers Scotland, Wildfowl and Wetland Trust, World Wildlife Fund and Zoological Society of London.

Authors:
Elena Blackmore, Ralph Underhill, Jamie McQuilkin, Rosie Leach, Tim Holmes.

Research:
Analysis: Netta Weinstein (University of Essex), Paul Chilton (University of Lancaster), David Furley (University of Central London), **Design:** Netta Weinstein (University of Essex), Paul Chilton (University of Lancaster), Anat Bardi (Royal Holloway, University of London), Tom Crompton (WWF-UK), Ruth Smyth (RSPB), Catriona Lennox (MCS); **Interviews:** Rosie Leach (PIRC).

Design and illustration:
Ultimate Holding Company.

First published in the United Kingdom 2013 by the Public Interest Research Centre.
Public Interest Research Centre is a company limited by guarantee.
Registered Charity No.: 266446.
Registered No.: 1112242.
Registered Office: Y Plas, Machynlleth, Wales, SY20 8ER.

Common Cause for Nature: A practical guide to values and frames in conservation is licensed under a Creative Commons Attribution-ShareAlike 3.0 Unported License by the Public Interest Research Centre. We actively encourage reproduction in all forms, by all means electronic, mechanical, recording or otherwise.

Printed on 100% recycled, FSC-approved paper using vegetable-based inks.

ISBN:
978-0-9503648-4-1

Acknowledgements:
We'd like to particularly thank Kathryn Balaam, Stephen Ballard, Mark Boyd, Helen Bryant, Phil Burfield, Rob Bushby, Sarah Christie, Adam Cormack, Ray Clark, Toby Clark, Amy Coyte, Tom Crompton, Laura Drake, Emma Edwards, Lauren Eyles, Simon Fairlie, Dale Harrison, Rich Hawkins, Paul Hetherington, Stephen Hinchley, Ant Jarrett, Kit Jones, Jasper Kenter, Heather McFarlane, Dan McLean, Anthony Morrow, Marina Pacheco, Sue Ranger, Kerry Riddell, Simon Sagg, Bec Sanderson, Matt Shardlow, Guy Shrubsole, Neil Sinden, Angelah Sparg, Sarah Thomas, Fiona Underhill, Rhiannon Wadeson, Morag Watson, Matt Williams, Sophie Wynne-Jones, the VINE group, and our countless workshop attendees and patient interviewees for their comments, thoughts, insightful ideas, helpful criticisms, and many hours of fascinating conversations.

Responsibility for any errors, omissions or mistakes lies solely, of course, with PIRC.

This guide offers recommendations for the conservation sector and others on how to ensure their work strengthens the values that motivate people to protect and enjoy nature. Part of a longer report produced in collaboration with 13 UK conservation organisations, it is based on original analysis of these groups' communications, workshop discussions, survey responses and in-depth interviews.

"In nature, nothing is perfect and everything is perfect. Trees can be contorted, bent in weird ways, and they're still beautiful."

Alice Walker

Contents

Summary

Psychologists, advertisers and politicians have long understood that we are not rational. The 'rational individual' does not exist; even the most scientific or logically minded are influenced by values and emotions. Marketers use this knowledge to sell products, appealing to whichever values do so most effectively: to our desire for status in selling cars; to our hedonism when selling holidays; and so on. When selling a particular product to a mass audience, this approach works well.

When the objective is broader—as it is when communicating about environmental issues—problems arise. When we appeal to a particular value, we do not simply affect a purchase decision: we also influence people's social and environmental behaviour as a whole. Appeals to self-interested goals—wealth, status and public image among them— can actually reduce our environmental concern.

The conservation sector has enjoyed many successes; but a vast range of indicators point to a natural world in decline, and public concern about the environment is at a 20-year low.[1] Something must change drastically if we are to stop the loss of wildlife or limit the impacts of climate change. If we want people to care about the natural world and act to protect it, we must promote values that motivate them to do so—and think very carefully before encouraging self-interest.

Based on information gleaned from across the sector and psychological research on human values, this guide aims to help conservation groups consider which kinds of values will help them achieve their goals.

Overview

We start with an overview of the report's recommendations.

Section 1

Explains what values are; how they motivate us to care and act; and how two kinds in particular (intrinsic and extrinsic) influence our attitudes towards the environment.

The section then details an analysis of 13 conservation organisations communications materials, and the values they promote.

Section 2

Explains the role of frames and framing in communication and describes the frames identified in our communications analysis. In particular, we consider the use of threats and monetary incentives, as well as the passive role audiences are frequently encouraged to adopt.

Section 3

Considers the work of the sector in conservation and outdoor activities, and how these experiences can affect people's values. We offer some suggestions about how organisations engage with the public, business, media and government, and what they campaign for.

We end with some general conclusions and suggestions for further reading.

Key Recommendations

When communicating about nature

Try to:
- Show how amazing nature is;
- Share the experience of the natural world;
- Talk about people, society and compassion as well as the natural world;
- Explain where and why things are going wrong;
- Encourage action and creativity.

Avoid:
- Relying on messages that emphasise threat and loss;
- Appealing to the desire for power and money;
- Attempts to motivate people with conflicting values.

When responding to the communications, policy or work of others

Question the language that is commonly used. Look at the phrases that are frequently used by government and media—what values are they likely to promote?

Don't reinforce unhelpful terms and ideas. Avoid repeating language that appeals to values related to self-interest.

Create new terms and ways to express ideas that foster environmental values.

Work together to spread these terms and ideas. Reframing the debate requires a concerted group effort.

When talking about your work

Be open about the values your organisation holds and why you feel your work is important.

When engaging people in nature:
- Create and promote accessible natural places;
- Encourage hands-on activity.

When lobbying decision-makers:
- Question the use of unhelpful or anti-environmental language;
- Be proactive and set the agenda: do not simply respond;
- Encourage decision-makers to experience hands-on conservation.

When engaging the media:
- Be aware of the implicit values in the language you use;
- Avoid framing issues in economic terms wherever possible;
- Think carefully before using celebrities.

When measuring success:
- Measure what matters: connection with nature, values and wellbeing;
- Don't focus solely on economic measures.

In your working practices:
- Encourage creativity;
- Talk about why you value nature at work.

Campaign on Common Causes:
- Consider new interventions that will strengthen intrinsic values;
- Work with other organisations.

Work together:
- Focus more on collective action;
- Try not to undermine others' efforts: avoid appeals to values related to self-interest, or language that impedes action on conservation.

Starling population
remaining

Starling population
decline

Long term monitoring by the British Trust for Ornithology (BTO) shows that starling numbers have fallen by 66% in Britain since the mid-1970s.

Section 1

Values in conservation communications

Why communicating the scale
of the problem is not enough

People aren't 'rational', emotions and values are crucial in determining how we process information.

Fear and threat can make us feel helpless. They can also backfire, making us more materialistic and less concerned about the environment.

This means that when communicating big, potentially shocking messages, organisations may inadvertently reduce their audience's motivation to act.

A great many NGOs rely on presenting 'the facts' to mobilise their audiences. They are not always successful, and are frequently left wondering why public awareness of environmental problems has failed to motivate public action. All too often, our messages seem to be met with apathy.

The problem is that we fail to take account of how human beings think, rather than how we would like them to think. Human beings do not respond straightforwardly to information, but rely on a complex mixture of memory, emotions and judgments about their priorities. The result is neither 'objective' nor logical.

Strongly negative messages can evoke feelings of terror or dismay—focusing our attention, and conveying a sense of importance, but also leaving us feeling disempowered, overwhelmed and paralysed ('it's too big a problem— what can I possibly do about it?'), and so less motivated to act. Instead, we frequently try to avoid these threats, or want to exert control elsewhere— often by chasing materialistic comforts, with largely negative effects on the environment.

Organisations should therefore take care when raising awareness—including of scary and depressing things—that audiences are not overwhelmed.[2]

How does this make you feel?

Values motivate change

Values motivate change

Values are important in conservation work, as they motivate us to act. They also affect our attitudes. Two kinds are particularly important:

i) Intrinsic values; strongly associated with behaviours that benefit the environment and society;

ii) Extrinsic values, which make people more self-interested and reduce their willingness to act on behalf of the environment.

The way we communicate and the way we work both influence people's values.

Researchers, working in over 80 countries, have found around 60 human values that seem to recur across cultures (see Figure 1, page 23). Pretty much everyone holds every one of these values, but to varying degrees.[3]

Researchers have also mapped the relationships between values (see Figures 1 & 2, pages 22 & 23). The closer one value is to another, the more likely they will be held strongly at the same time (a person who prioritises protecting the environment is also likely to prioritise equality, for instance).

By contrast, the further apart any two values lie, the less likely we are to prioritise both of them at the same time (we are unlikely to prioritise both wealth and equality simultaneously). These relationships can also be mapped in a circle, as in Figure 2.

Two groups of values are especially important in conservation work: intrinsic (*self-direction, benevolence* and *universalism*) and extrinsic values (*power* and *achievement*).

Figure 2
Simplified values circumplex

Figure 1
Values map

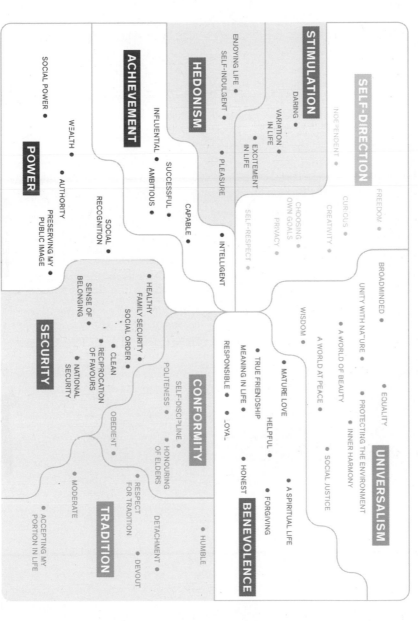

INTRINSIC VALUES

EXTRINSIC VALUES

SELF-DIRECTION

INDEPENDENT •

FREEDOM •

CURIOUS •

CREATIVITY •

CHOOSING
OWN GOALS •

PRIVACY •

SELF-RESPECT •

STIMULATION

DARING •

VARIATION
IN LIFE •

EXCITEMENT
IN LIFE •

HEDONISM

ENJOYING LIFE •

SELF-INDULGENT •

PLEASURE •

INTELLIGENT •

ACHIEVEMENT

INFLUENTIAL •

AMBITIOUS •

SUCCESSFUL •

CAPABLE •

SOCIAL
RECOGNITION •

POWER

SOCIAL POWER •

WEALTH •

AUTHORITY •

PRESERVING MY
PUBLIC IMAGE •

UNIVERSALISM

BROADMINDED •

UNITY WITH NATURE •

EQUALITY •

PROTECTING THE ENVIRONMENT •

INNER HARMONY •

A WORLD OF BEAUTY •

A WORLD AT PEACE •

WISDOM •

SOCIAL JUSTICE •

MATURE LOVE •

BENEVOLENCE

TRUE FRIENDSHIP •

HELPFUL •

A SPIRITUAL LIFE •

RESPONSIBLE •

MEANING IN LIFE •

OYA •

FORGIVING •

HONEST •

CONFORMITY

POLITENESS •

SELF-DISCIPLINE •

HONOURING
OF ELDERS •

RESPECT
FOR TRADITION •

DETACHMENT •

DEVOUT •

HUMBLE •

TRADITION

MODERATE •

ACCEPTING MY
PORTION IN LIFE •

SECURITY

HEALTHY •

FAMILY SECURITY •

SOCIAL ORDER •

SENSE OF
BELONGING •

CLEAN •

RECIPROCATION
OF FAVOURS •

NATIONAL
SECURITY •

OBEDIENT •

Why do values matter in conservation work?

If a person prioritises intrinsic values, like equality or unity with nature, research has consistently found that they are more likely to express concern for the environment and other people.

Those that prioritise extrinsic values such as power and wealth are less likely to be concerned about nature and other people.

It is important to remember that most people hold each of these values to some degree. Values are not character types: there are no fully 'extrinsic' or 'intrinsic' people. We are all a combination of both.

Experiments have found that values can be temporarily 'engaged', making people more likely to act on them. After reading words related to equality and fairness (intrinsic values), we are more likely to volunteer than after reading words related to power and ambition (extrinsic values).[4]

The opposition effect

When one value is engaged, we are likely to suppress opposing values, making them appear less important.

Intrinsic and extrinsic values are like two balloons connected to each other—as one expands, the other contracts.

If you reflect for a few minutes on wealth and status, for instance, you are likely become less motivated to act in an environmentally friendly way.

Intrinsic values are engaged, likely suppressing extrinsic values (top), or extrinsic values are engaged, likely suppressing intrinsic values (middle). Engaging both at once can create mental discomfort (bottom).

The spillover effect

By engaging one value, we can also engage values that are close to it. Reading words related to equality, for instance, can thus engage protecting the environment and broadmindedness. We call this the spillover effect.

For example, one study found that, after thinking briefly about the importance of broadmindedness, affiliation, and self-acceptance (intrinsic values), people rated climate change and the loss of the British countryside as more important than did another group asked to think about extrinsic values. Importantly, no mention of the environment was made.[5]

Our experiences shape our values

When we engage values repeatedly, they become entrenched in people's minds. People become predisposed to regard them as important. In this way, everything we experience influences our values.

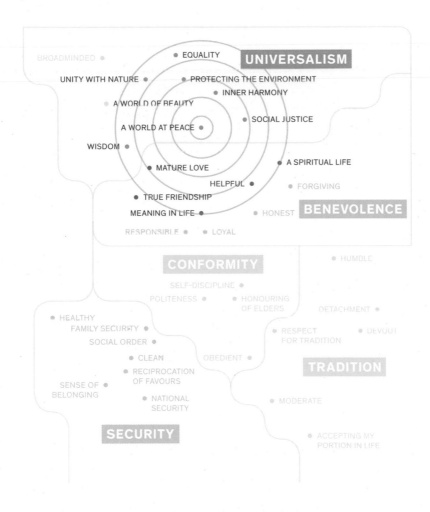

What do you value most?

What does your organisation value?

What values are nature organisations communicating now?

"As a valued customer, we like to keep you up to date and informed about product news and special offers."

"Get creative in the forest!"

What values are nature organisations communicating now?

Examining six months-worth of external communications of 13 conservation organisations, we analysed the values these expressed and frames that they used.

The results are presented below. The graph shows how often each value was expressed; the coloured boxes provide examples.

Intrinsic messages
Motivate concern about the environment

Universalism:
Understanding, appreciation, tolerance and protection for the welfare of all people and for nature.

Examples of how universalism was expressed in communications:
- 'Nature is amazing—let's keep it that way.'
- 'I know that you share our vision of a future in which people and nature thrive alongside one another.'
- 'This is the first step to creating a generation who care for each other and the natural world and understand the ways in which we can help to protect the planet by minimising our impact.'

Benevolence:
Preservation and enhancement of the welfare of people with whom one is in frequent personal contact.

Examples of appeals to benevolence:
- 'You're no longer a visitor... you're one of the team.'
- 'Enjoy time with friends and family, learn more about your local area and even look after the environment.'
- 'We want to help local authorities and developers work to give everyone equal access to green spaces and all the benefits that go with them.'

Self-direction:
Independent thought and action—choosing, creating, exploring.

Examples of appeals to self-direction:
- 'Discover new areas near you, meet new people and enjoy the beautiful winter scenery.'
- 'Get creative in the forest.'
- 'Take action.'
- 'My true nature is an inspiring creative project that invites young people to reflect on what nature means to them and why it's important.'

Full Results

Achievement:
Personal success through demonstrating competence according to social standards.

Examples of appeals to achievement:
○ 'An aspiring... competition.'
○ 'It is not good enough to take a 'laissez-faire' approach to planning.'
○ 'If we want to achieve and expect the right kind of economic growth...?'
○ 'The campaign also gained [organisation] a great deal of publicity with appearances on and in regional TV, radio stations and newspapers.'

Power:
Social status and prestige, control or dominance over people and resources.

Examples of power in communications:
○ 'We're freezing our prices for 2011, and with no VAT to pay on tickets, that all adds up to big day out at a surprisingly small price.'
○ 'You can help by buying (or even selling) tickets, and there's a £5,000 top prize!'
○ 'Utilising... assets and resources to generate funds.'
○ '[You will receive] a subscription to our award-winning... magazine and priority access to... events. With exclusive behind-the-scenes access...'

Try to:
Encourage people to explore and be creative. In the communications analysed, there were many appeals to intrinsic self-direction values (independent thought and action, exploring/creating). This is positive and should be pursued further.

Talk about how amazing nature is, and why it needs protection. Don't just ask for help: tell people why. Many people love the countryside and wildlife, and these motivations can be engaged before launching straight into appeals. Avoid 'Will you help us save animals from extinction?' before '...wildlife is amazing, and something we should all enjoy together.'

Talk about people. There are many ways to engage intrinsic motivations, including appeals to community, loyalty, fairness and tolerance, all of which are likely to motivate concern for the environment (see pages 26 & 27, on the spillover effect).

Talk openly about your organisation's values. This will engage and help strengthen intrinsic values.

Avoid:
Appeals to competition, status or money (extrinsic values). They are likely to make people less motivated to act on behalf of the environment.

Results are discussed in more detail in the full report.

Conflicting messages

About a quarter of messages that contained values placed opposing
values together.

Examples
Power, achievement, universalism and benevolence:
'We run a weekly lottery with a jackpot of £1,000... And there's a rollover
prize... up to £8,000!... [W]e rely on you to fund our work and as I said
before, we're incredibly grateful for your generosity... Your support will
help to preserve our natural heritage for future generations to enjoy.'

Power, achievement, universalism and benevolence:
'As well as being in with a chance of winning a cash prize, you'll also have
the satisfaction of knowing that you're doing more to help us protect
birds, their habitats and the wider environment.'

The idea that appealing to a range of values will motivate more people is
likely mistaken: placing intrinsic and extrinsic messages together can cause
mental 'dissonance' or discomfort, and reduce people's motivation.

→ **Recommendation**

Avoid using values that clash—wealth alongside protecting the environment,
for instance. This can cause confusion (see page 24) and is unlikely to
motivate people.

Audience segmentation

We are often advised to 'meet your audience where they are', normally with the implication that we must appeal to the extrinsic values of the public. But researchers find that people usually consider intrinsic values—especially benevolence (concern for those with whom you have close personal contact)—most important, while only a small minority prioritise extrinsic values (such as wealth, image and success). This seems to hold true across a wide range of cultures: one study found benevolence was the most prioritised value in over 60 countries, with universalism and self-direction usually in second and third place.[6]

This may be surprising, as concern for material goods and monetary achievement seem so widespread in our society. However, behind these concerns, people are generally motivated by the welfare of others. Moreover, because we all hold every value to some extent, people who generally prioritise extrinsic goals will also value intrinsic goals. 'Meeting people where they are' does not have to mean reinforcing their self-interest.

UK values

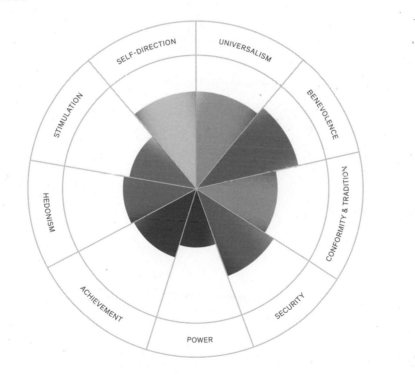

Do nature organisations segment their audiences?

We found some variation in the communications aimed at different audiences.

In communications aimed at members and supporters, there were more appeals to power values than in communications aimed at the general public.

Members and supporters

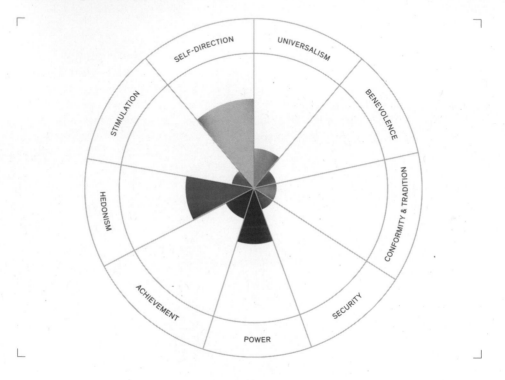

In communications aimed at the general public. There were more appeals
to self-direction, hedonism and stimulation words than in communications
for members and supporters or for business and government.

General public

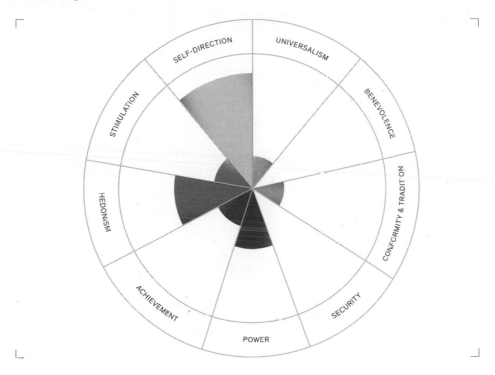

In communications aimed at business and government, there were fewer appeals to intrinsic values, and more frequent appeals to power values, wealth in particular.

Business and government

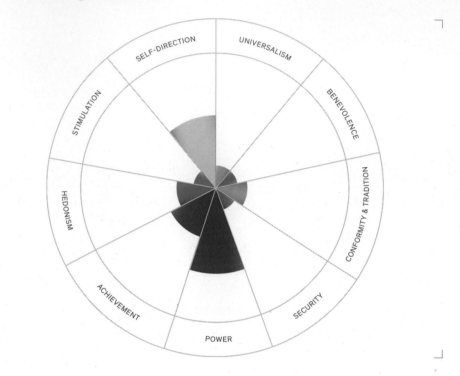

Tailoring messages to different audiences should not mean appealing to extrinsic values. Communications should vary depending on the audience—civil servants might not be approached in exactly the same way as the general public—but where possible, communication with any audience should foster intrinsic values.

With government audiences, for instance, the emphasis could be on the feelings of an organisation's membership: *'We speak for our membership who feel strongly that wildlife and the natural world is incredibly important... nature benefits us all in a way that simply cannot be expressed in purely monetary terms.'*

Of course, appeals to intrinsic values do not always have to mention the environment! Mentioning social justice, peace, affiliation and independence can increase environmental concern indirectly via the spillover effect (see pages 26 & 27).

**How do you communicate
in your work?**

**Do you recognise the
issues highlighted?**

**How do you think your work
might impact on values?**

Section 2
Frames in conservation communications

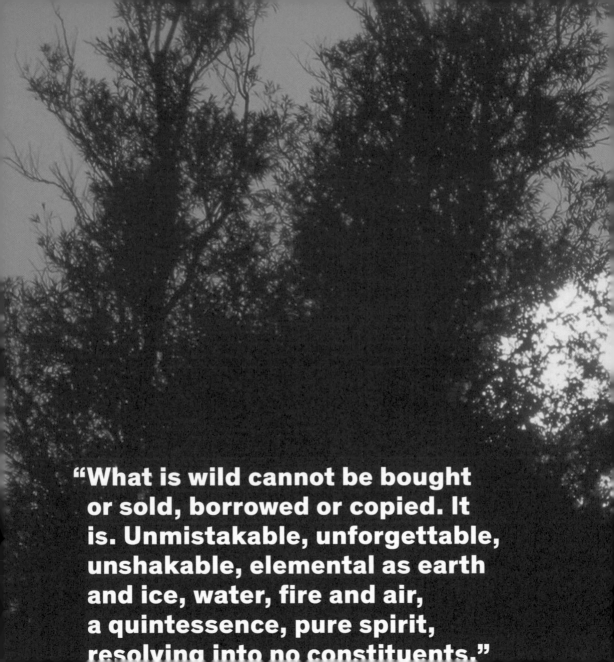

"What is wild cannot be bought
or sold, borrowed or copied. It
is. Unmistakable, unforgettable,
unshakable, elemental as earth
and ice, water, fire and air,
a quintessence, pure spirit,
resolving into no constituents."

Frames in conservation communications

Frames are how we connect with values through language.

Organisations should be aware of commonly-used frames that promote environmentally unhelpful values.

When we hear the word 'nature' we might think of 'trees', 'animals', 'the outdoors', or of particular memories and emotions. These associations will be evoked even if we are not consciously aware of it. Every word or concept is mentally connected to a number of associated words, memories, emotions and values. This set of associations is known as a frame.

Switching words and phrases—or creating different associations between concepts (through metaphor, for instance)—can really influence the way we understand a situation. Presenting the same information in a different way will change how people think, feel and respond.

→ Consumers and citizens

In an experiment, two groups of volunteers were given an identical task—labelled either a Consumer Reaction Task or Citizen Reaction Task. The 'consumers' became more competitive and less likely to engage in collective action (such as volunteering to join a group). They also conserved less water in a resource management game, and felt less personal responsibility for environmental problems.[7]

Consider some of the different ways of framing conservation ideas:

- 'the outdoors' vs. 'the countryside'?
- 'public investment' or 'taxpayers' money'?
- 'wildlife' or 'biodiversity'?

Imagine if the government's 'biodiversity offset' process was instead framed as 'compensation for damage to wildlife.'

On the following page, we outline how an organisation might respond to an existing frame: in this case, the Government's Red Tape Challenge.

Organisations will often be required to respond to frames created by others. In doing so, it may be worth asking the following questions:

1. **What values does the frame appeal to?**

2. **Do you need to respond to it?**

3. **Can you challenge it?**

4. **Can you create an alternative?**

The Red Tape Challenge

The Red Tape Challenge is a government initiative to reduce legislation (a 'raft of regulations'), which is presented as a burden that 'hurt[s] business, doing real damage to our economy.'[8]

1. What values does the frame appeal to?

Legislation is presented as a bureaucratic barrier that needs to be removed. The key actor is the private sector, implying that business interests are paramount ('This has hurt business'). This appears to promote power and wealth (extrinsic concerns) as key priorities.

While the Government might claim it wishes to cut only 'inefficient' pieces of legislation, the 'challenge' aspect suggests the removal of as much 'red tape' as possible. Imagine how different the response may have been to a simple 'review of existing legislation'.

2. Do you need to respond?

Participating in this consultation risks promoting and strengthening the negative frame. Fail to participate, however, and environmental concerns might not be defended.

3. Can you challenge the frame?

We could avoid using the language of government and challenge it wherever possible—in letters, consultation responses and face-to-face meetings. We might state, for example, 'If this is to be a fair, evidence-based review it should not use language that portrays legislation as an unnecessary barrier.'

4. Can you create an alternative?

A new, intrinsic frame could strengthen opposition to damaging attempts to remove environmental safeguards. When constructing an alternative, it may be possible to:

○ Focus on intrinsic concerns for people and nature:

'We in the UK are very lucky to have so many amazing habitats and species, and laws that benefit both them and us. Our government's decisions should reflect the concern most people feel for wildlife—and ensure that everyone can enjoy the benefits of connecting with nature.'

○ Reframe the debate as positive rather than negative:

'There has been a groundswell of public support for new laws ensuring people can thrive in harmony with nature.'

○ Reframe 'red tape' as 'green foundations':

'Support our green foundations—laws that make sure people and wildlife are looked after.'

Creating new frames: recommendations

It will be difficult to challenge the frames that government and media use, because they are constantly being reinforced. Conservation groups will need to work together to change them—possibly through umbrella organisations such as Wildlife and Countryside Link.

"You cannot get through a single day without having an impact on the world around you. What you do makes a difference, and you have to decide what kind of difference you want to make."

Jane Goodall

How do conservation organisations use frames?

How do conservation organisations use frames?

How were issues framed in the communications analysed?

Connection to nature
and discovery

Consumer and
transaction frames

Ecosystem
services

Conservation NGO
as superhero

Passive
supporter

Ignoring
causes

Threat

Connection to nature and discovery

These intrinsic frames communicate our positive experiences of the natural world. Conservation groups should consider using them more often.

Connection to nature

Organisations sometimes used frames depicting people as connected with nature:

'Our vision is of a world where [animals] and people thrive together.'

'When we contemplate the whole globe...'

'...to build a future in which humans live in harmony with nature.'

→ Awe-some

Experiences or images that evoke awe—a jaw—dropping view of snow-capped mountain ranges, or a murmuration of starlings at dusk—can have a major impact. Researchers find that awe expands our perception of time, and makes us more patient, less materialistic, happier and more willing to help others.[9]

Engage intrinsic values *(unity with nature, protecting the environment)* by sharing personal experiences and provoking feelings of awe, using pictures of landscapes, wildlife, gardens, urban green spaces and so on.

Exploration and enjoyment

Frames that focus on outdoor activities—'walking', 'adventure', 'exploration', and 'discovery', are likely to promote self-direction, universalism and stimulation values.

When discussing fun and pleasure, however—as many of these frames did— care should be taken to avoid more extrinsic values related to self-interest.

→ Recommendations

Frames that focus on connecting with nature are strongly linked to intrinsic values, which help promote pro-environmental and pro-social behaviours. Try to use them often.

Avoid focusing on individual benefits:
'Pamper yourself, safe in the knowledge that all the ingredients are good for the planet and good for you.'

'...enjoy feeling good knowing you're helping save a species.'

Concentrate on what makes the outdoors and nature inspiring:
'This truly is a wildlife spectacle—a blizzard of wings, a mass of black and white and a cacophony of sound.'

'A day of adventure.'

'Discover new areas near you, meet new people and enjoy the beautiful winter scenery.'

On other intrinsic activities in the natural world:
'...bring people closer to nature using a unique combination of the arts and nature.'

And on our connection with nature:
'...this brilliant world we all share.'

Consumer and transaction frames

Treating the public and your supporters as customers is likely to make them more self-interested and less likely to take action for nature.

Organisations often used a 'commercial transaction' frame, depicting their audience as 'consumers' buying products from a 'retailer'. Sometimes this was implicit: people could buy membership in return for goods (posters, toys, entrance to visitor sites), for instance. In many cases, transactional frames almost entirely overshadowed any emphasis on nature conservation.

Worryingly, this frame is related to extrinsic 'power' values (particularly wealth), which tend to suppress environmental concern and action.

Examples from the texts

'The [animals] have proved their pulling power in our shops, as more than 10,000... products have been sold.'

'As a valued customer, we like to keep you up to date and informed about product news and special offers.'

'Buy online & save 10%.'

'We're freezing our prices for 2011, and with no VAT to pay on tickets, that all adds up to big day out at a surprisingly small price.'

'Save Nature while you shop!'

Conservation organisations rely heavily on donations and cannot escape talking about money, but should try to avoid framing donations as transactions, or focusing on what people can get for themselves.

Avoid using gifts and prizes as incentives, or offering 'money-off' memberships, which evoke a 'consumer' relationship.

Try framing membership and donations as joining a community working to improve the environment and making space for wildlife.

If you do want to offer things, try thinking about experiences (access to nature) or educational materials that are likely to encourage people to spend more time in nature and appeal to people's intrinsic values.

Also see Example: 'Give as you Live' app, page 85.

Ecosystem services

Organisations could consider talking more about the public benefits of nature and less about the monetary value of ecosystems.

The benefits of nature

Many communications focused on the services nature provides:

'...provide health benefits...'

'...protect Britain's walking environments and promote the healthy, social and environmental benefits of walking to all.'

Most examples linked social and environmental benefits, and appealed to intrinsic values, including self-direction (autonomous activity), universalism (unity with nature), and benevolence (concern for the wellbeing of others).

Economic valuation

'Even thinking in monetary terms about environmental resources and 'nature' may discourage collective thinking and promote individualist behaviour.'[10]

Gabrielle Horup, 2011

Other frames pointed out the economic benefits of ecosystems ('good for [the environment]; good for the economy'; 'how restoring nature makes us wealthier').

Economic language might sometimes seem appropriate—when responding to government budget decisions, for instance—but it makes it more difficult to use moral language in future; risks undermining public concern by reinforcing power values; and helps normalise economic framing elsewhere (when discussing the 'cost' of social care, for instance).[11]

→ **Recommendation**

Where possible, avoid economic frames. Where they are unavoidable, begin by discussing the real benefits—to society and the environment—and make clear that monetary benefits are a means to an end. Point out that the social and environmental benefits are linked.

Superhero and passive supporter frames

Conservation groups too often give passive roles to the public and their members, while portraying themselves as superheroes sorting out problems on behalf of others.

Motivate people by portraying them as active and involved, not just passive sources of income.

The superhero frame

A defender/rescuer frame frequently portrayed conservation groups as heroic: 'protecting' or 'safeguarding' a victim ('fragile', 'dependent', 'critically endangered' landscapes and ecosystems) from danger or crisis ('disastrous impacts'; 'threat').

The frame is problematic because it relies on threat and fear. The organisation is an all-powerful superhero and the audience is a passive and inferior helper. This is disempowering—reducing both an audience's sense of agency and the motivation for more active involvement.

Passive people

Portraying your audiences as passive supporters is unlikely to motivate more active involvement. Instead, encourage participation and note opportunities for action.

→ **Recommendations**

Avoid saying: 'We are the only ones protecting the critically vulnerable [species]—without us, they will be extinct within a few years. You can assist our valiant efforts today by donating £3.'

Instead, describe the relationship as a more equal partnership, and present opportunities to participate: 'Together we can protect this species for the longer term'; 'as a community of people who care about this issue, there are a number of actions we can take to help'

Talking about why and avoiding threat

Conservation organisations rarely explain the root of the problem. This can cause confusion—and organisations could think about trying to explain the causes better.

However, it is also important not to rely too heavily on threatening messages. Where such messages are unavoidable, balance them with information about how positive opportunities for actions fit into the larger picture of addressing a problem.

Talking about why

Organisations might avoid talking about the causes of problems because they assume people already know, or because they are concerned about such explanations (or the solutions) being challenging to their audience. This approach may be problematic. Without a clear causal relationship, it is difficult to process what an appropriate response may be. Some conservation problems are complicated and difficult to articulate, but communicators should find ways of discussing them (see Case Study: DEFRA, page 64 & 65).

Even if people are aware of the root cause of a problem, if the solution or action being suggested is not of a similar scale to the problem it may cause confusion. For example, we are told climate change will have catastrophic effects, but are only asked to turn our thermostat down a degree or two (rather than more concerted action to reduce our environmental impact). This can also reduce motivation in the longer term.[12]

Talking about threat

Threat and fear can be unhelpful: when people feel overwhelmed and unable to act, they can become less motivated, and even more materialistic. By contrast, positive messages may be less shocking or attention-grabbing, but are likely to spur action and foster creativity (particularly when they evoke self-direction values). This doesn't mean that there isn't a place for negative messages—sometimes we need to talk about the severity of a situation.

→ Recommendations

Highlight the causes of a problem. However, this must be balanced against relying too heavily on threat—try placing the emphasis in communications on intrinsic, positive solutions. Explain how the actions being asked for fit into this larger picture.

Use less of:
'...extinction is a real and terrible possibility.'

'Right now, the [animal] is in desperate trouble.'

'Our area is in danger.'

And try balancing negative messages with:
'It can be very easy to feel powerless in situations like this, but it is important to remember that deforestation can be halted.'

'Make [your] own 'stand' against a planning proposal.'

'Giving pupils a voice and enabling them to take action on sustainability...'

Department for Environment, Food and Rural Affairs (DEFRA) on biodiversity loss

→ Talking about threat, why, and balancing this with positive action

Text taken from DEFRA website.

'Our planet and its ecosystems supply us with all the natural resources we need to survive—essentials like clean air, water, food and fuel. Contact with nature is good for our physical and mental health.' This highlights the benefits we receive from nature in an intrinsic way—although more focus could have been put on our attachment and connection with nature.

'Biodiversity—the variety of life on earth—is declining, with up to a third of all animals threatened with extinction. Climate change is contributing to this decline, causing the diversity of life to be lost at a faster rate than ever before. A 1°C rise in global temperatures threatens the survival of 10% of these species.' Here, the text could have also talked about the causes of climate change in brief, for example: 'The scale of climate change we are currently seeing is largely caused by human energy and resource use.'

'Our wildlife areas are too disjointed and fragmented, which makes it harder for wildlife to flourish and respond to climate change and other pressures, like pollution.' This could also have mentioned reasons for fragmented wildlife areas—such as the built environment or agriculture.

'All countries need to act to improve biodiversity and preserve natural ecosystems. Otherwise the natural environment, wildlife and human life as we know it are all at risk.' The text continues by discussing the action—international agreements, for instance—that may be needed to address climate change. Whilst it highlights the need for action, it risks being disempowering by focusing only on government-level action and focusing on a highly threatening message. A message that would be more likely to motivate would be one that highlighted the positive opportunities for protecting the natural world, and actions that could also be taken at individual and community levels, such as: 'Together, in our communities, we can also act to improve our local areas.' However, this was likely outside of the perceived remit of the author.

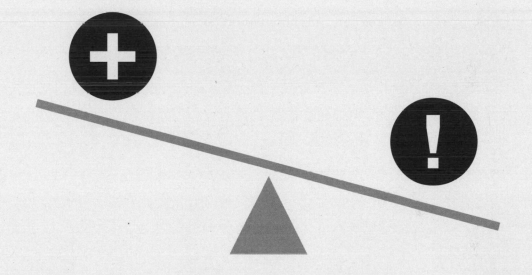

Do you recognise these frames in conservation communications?

Does your organisation commonly use any of the frames mentioned?

Can you think of other frames you use, and what values they might appeal to?

Section 3
Values in other areas of conservation work

Values in other areas of conservation work

Values are promoted by experiences as well as communications.

Over time, these experiences can strengthen or weaken particular values.

Take care that the experiences you create—including through the policies you help bring into being—promote helpful values.

Like communications, experiences influence our values. For example, consumer experiences like high-street shopping are likely to foster materialism and sap environmental concern.

Over time, our values are strengthened by society—from the policies and institutions we encounter to our education; from the media we consume to our experience of nature.

This means it is not just the campaigning or fundraising materials organisations produce that influence their audience's values. The wider experiences an organisation creates in its reserves, volunteering schemes or through policy changes it successfully demands will also have an impact.

The following sections explore the implications of values in several areas:

**Engaging
the public**

**Influencing
government**

**Engaging with
the media**

**Working with
business**

**Measuring
success**

**Our working
practices**

To help foster helpful values and limit the spread of unhelpful values, conservation groups should also consider:

**Campaigning
on values**

**Working
together**

SPIRITUALITY

TRADITIONS

CULTURE

COMMUNITY

RELIGION

SOCIAL NORMS

CELEBRITY

INTERNET USE

SENSATIONALISM

PRINT MEDIA

MEDIA

ADVERTISING

OUR VALUES ARE SHAPED BY OUR
LIVED EXPERIENCE

MORAL PANICS

CULTURAL DIFFERENCES

PLACE AND SPACE

PETS

HOME

PARENTS' BELIEFS

PARENTHOOD

HOME ENVIRONMENT

MIGRATION

FAMILY

URBAN VS RURAL

TRADITIONAL OR PROGRESSIVE

SUPPORTIVE OR CONTROLLING

PLANTS

COUNTRY

ANIMALS

PUNISHMENTS

STATE OR PRIVATE

NATURE

TREES

EDUCATION

TIME IN EDUCATION

RELIGIOUS

BUSINESS

OUTDOOR ACTIVITIES

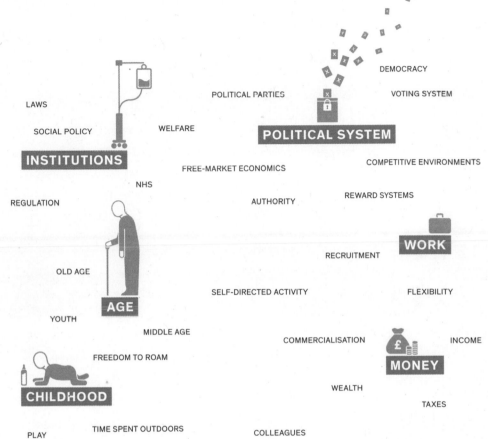

LAWS

SOCIAL POLICY

WELFARE

INSTITUTIONS

POLITICAL PARTIES

DEMOCRACY

VOTING SYSTEM

POLITICAL SYSTEM

FREE-MARKET ECONOMICS

COMPETITIVE ENVIRONMENTS

NHS

REGULATION

AUTHORITY

REWARD SYSTEMS

WORK

RECRUITMENT

OLD AGE

SELF-DIRECTED ACTIVITY

FLEXIBILITY

AGE

YOUTH

MIDDLE AGE

COMMERCIALISATION

INCOME

MONEY

FREEDOM TO ROAM

CHILDHOOD

WEALTH

TAXES

PLAY

TIME SPENT OUTDOORS

COLLEAGUES

CIVIL RIGHTS

HOBBIES

OCCUPY

SOCIAL LIFE

SOCIAL MOVEMENTS

CLUBS

PEER GROUPS

CAMPAIGNS

FEMINIST GROUPS

GAY RIGHTS

FRIENDS

GENERATIONAL COHORT

CHALLENGES AND ARGUMENTS

"Places matter. Their rules, their scale, their design include or exclude civil society, pedestrianism, equality, diversity (economic and otherwise), understanding of where water comes from and garbage goes, consumption or conservation. They map our lives."

Rebecca Solnit

Engaging the public

The disconnection of children—and adults—from nature has attracted considerable concern. An understanding of values raises further concerns, since our experience of nature helps strengthen intrinsic values, fostering concern for others as well as the natural world.

Places, sites and reserves

'Even nature itself has become a commodity. Many believe they cannot experience it unless they are in a nature reserve, have the right pair of binoculars, or are wearing the correctly endorsed clothes... So often nature is seen as something to travel to—not something we are immersed in all the time and dependent upon for our physical, emotional and spiritual health.'[13]

The *Natural Childhood* report

Natural spaces are important places for people to explore nature and learn about wildlife. They need to be more accessible, and the experience of nature should be integrated into people's everyday lives. This may mean rethinking the traditional view of 'sites' and 'reserves'.

→ **Case study: Stalled Spaces**

A city-wide initiative in Glasgow presents an innovative approach to tackling the poor environmental conditions the economic downturn has created. Stalled Spaces helps promote public health and strengthen communities by repurposing vacant or under-used land as urban growing spaces, community gardens, wildflower meadows, mountain-bike trails and sculpture parks.

Its projects encourage harmony with nature, while their accessibility reinforces equality and social justice values. These are all universalism values, likely to increase concern for nature and other people—strengthening communities and environmental behaviours.

Active members

If someone visits your organisation's website and clicks 'get involved', what are they presented with? What roles are available? Try this on your own organisation's website, and find out!

Some organisations encourage active conservation; others ask only—or mostly—for money.

Some people might not be able to involve themselves more actively, due to time, mobility or family commitments; but many others could be much more active if given the opportunity and encouragement!

Volunteering is a great way of reinforcing intrinsic values, as are many activities like it. Helping volunteers design campaigns and take action together will help strengthen intrinsic values, such as creativity, community and affiliation. Other actions—encouraging the use of public transport, for example—can be environmentally beneficial at the same time.

Compass is an online tool designed to get more people involved with Greenpeace. 1,200 people from 116 countries have already signed up, taking part in brainstorming sessions, debates, online workshops, the crafting of campaigns, the designing of posters, writing scripts for adverts and advising on organisational strategy. In the words of Martin Lloyd, who worked on the project, *'You start to get the idea that there is a lot of untapped potential there.'* Compass revealed an appetite for different and unusual forms of engagement, such as calls for political advocacy in places where this uncommon.

→ Case study: The Conservation Volunteers

Volunteering is a good way for people to learn about conservation, take part, forge communities and connect with nature.[14]

Spending time outdoors and with others can strengthen intrinsic values (concern for nature and people) and encourage more active involvement.

Volunteering can foster sociability and a sense of confidence that hugely benefit people's mental health. As one volunteer reported of their experience in conservation (an experience that is frequently reported): *'From earlier years I wasn't confident, I had mental issues. You name it I had it, I was always angry, always depressed; shy. People here gave me the confidence to stop me losing it. I never knew how to talk to anyone you know? I used to be racist, sexist, everything. I would offend god knows how many people. I didn't mean to, I didn't know any better... I just said wrong things all the time. I've gained respect from people now, I can get out of bed without feeling totally miserable every morning, I mean I even get out of bed! I can say what's good and what's bad, I know now. I can open up to people, talk to them about my problems, I could talk before, at people, but I couldn't talk to people, know what I mean? Tell you what, now if I need to hand out leaflets door-to-door I can do that, I can talk to people I don't even know! When I started with this my whole life changed, what we're doing here is good.'*

→ **Recommendations**

Consider supporting and creating more urban green spaces and reserves, perhaps collaborating with existing community, school and environmental groups.

Encourage more hands-on connection with nature at existing reserves and sites (see The Conservation Volunteers, opposite page).

Work together to get people outdoors. Collectively, the sector could create an online portal where people across the country can access details about all its many projects, sites, and events. This would provide a good resource for people to find the easiest ways to connect with nature, whether at a reserve, park, or city farm. It could also be used to identify areas where access to nature is lacking.

Address barriers to outdoor activity, such as road safety.

Offer a variety of ways to get involved: lead with the more active 'volunteer' or 'take action'; keep 'join' or 'donate' further down the list.

Help volunteers collaborate to create their own campaigns and actions.

Create toolkits for community action.

Organisations should make sure that volunteers' experiences embody and reinforce intrinsic values wherever possible.

- Make volunteering inclusive and diverse;
- Emphasise its social and community aspects to strengthen intrinsic motivation;
- Encourage creativity and autonomy, and be open to questions;
- Reinforcing self-direction values will strengthen people's motivation to act, as well as their own feelings of self-respect;
- Allow people to interact with nature wherever possible.

Influencing government

As conservation organisations have become more professional, governments have taken them more seriously. Green NGOs are now seen as legitimate stakeholders in many areas of policy—but many wonder whether access to this 'inside track' has come at too high a cost.

Reframing the debate

Governments are frequently able to frame policy debates, forcing the conservation sector into a reactive rather than proactive role. Adopting the economic valuation of nature is an example of this, which is likely to be problematic (see pages 60 & 61).

Setting the agenda

Many organisations focus intensely on official processes such as consultations or parliamentary bills. This is generally a reactive process, since asking for something not already on the government's agenda is seen as politically naïve.

Nevertheless, if the existing agenda will not achieve sufficient or lasting changes, the sector should think about pushing for bigger changes. Even if unsuccessful, these campaigns would create strong frames, raising public awareness and reinforcing intrinsic values.

Getting decision-makers outdoors

Because frames are transmitted not only through language but also through context, intrinsic values become easier to express and more convincing in natural surroundings. Many conservation organisations have therefore tried hard to get decision-makers outdoors—taking them to the Itchin River or Capercaillie-watching, to name only two examples.

The demands on people's time might make these events difficult to organise, but make every effort to do so: they are likely to reinforce the intrinsic values of decision-makers.

Question the language used by government. Whether at a meeting or in a consultation response, avoid reinforcing extrinsic frames.

Wildlife and Countryside Link could establish a group that focuses on framing. This could assess the values and frames associated with policy discussions and suggest alternative language for conservation NGOs to use.

Senior staff from different organisations could meet regularly to discuss the values implications of their current activities and the language being used.

Establish positive campaigns celebrating wildlife to encourage the public to feel more strongly about protecting it. If species and habitats are always perceived as threatened, people may start to feel helpless and demotivated.

Work together to identify effective, long-term policy solutions. Where these are not currently on the political agenda, collaborative efforts (such as the *Natural Childhood* initiative) can help shift the debate.

Consider the places in which decision-makers are being engaged—as these, too will engage particular values. Where possible, increase opportunities to expose them to the decisions you want them to make—outdoors, or viewing the impacts on the natural environment.

Engaging with the media

The media is key in creating and strengthening frames.

Think carefully about the values that media coverage will be appealing to.

Media coverage plays a large role in extending the reach of conservation messages. The media is instrumental in creating frames in public debate, and reading this coverage may be the only time some audiences think about conservation. This makes it important to think about the language used. The 'reach' (uptake by mainstream papers, for instance) is not the only consideration; another will be what frames and values are being promoted, and whether these are helpful to motivating conservation concern and action.

As discussed in the Red Tape Challenge example (see pages 50 & 51), organisations may want to think about challenging the most commonly—used frame, or adding another perspective. When opposing the 'Challenge', environmental organisations had a high media presence in getting their concerns heard. However, many organisations repeated the government framing (prioritising business needs over human and environmental needs), and some made their case on the economic benefits of laws that provided environmental protection: two strategies that may engage extrinsic values.

Shaping environmental stories to fit the news agenda may therefore not always be the best tactic: organisations may instead wish to think about how to help shift the debate onto their own, intrinsic terms.

Making a splash

We've discussed the use of 'shock tactics' earlier in this guide. Provoking feelings of threat, fear or loss may successfully raise the profile of an issue. However, rather than motivating action, these feelings may leave people feeling helpless and increasingly demotivated, or even inclined to actively avoid the issue. In meeting the media's appetite for such stories, organisations may also be unwittingly perpetuating the focus on negative stories.

In these cases, organisations may wish to think about what the intrinsic parts of these stories are and how to highlight positive action to address an issue. This may mean thinking carefully before using media messages that focus on scary or depressing things. If people only hear messages of extinction and the threat of environmental damage, they may only associate conservation with loss. Frames and associations around enhancing our connection with nature and celebration of the things we care about are more likely to motivate action.

The case of ash dieback in 2012 received considerable press attention. This was doubtless partly because it tapped into some deeply-held public emotions around loss of British species and the countryside, and partly because of the high 'shock' factor of the possibility of losing so many trees so quickly. Concern was often framed around intrinsic values: our emotional connection with nature and the failure to protect something so important to people. Whilst there was little to be done to save the ash trees, there were a number of good interventions in the debate—including calls to make sure more protection was afforded other tree species. Such activities reinforce the perception that there are still actions which can be taken to protect nature, and that we should take this as a learning experience. There was also media attention focused on events held around the country to say 'farewell' to the trees. These stories highlight how important people think nature is, and that people can create a sense of community and affiliation around this shared sense of importance. These initiatives also promote self-direction and agency by highlighting self-organising groups of people.

Celebrity involvement

Celebrities can grab the attention of the public and media, and help reach new audiences; but their involvement can also help reinforce extrinsic values, particularly if they are known for their wealth, status or public image. In the short term, you may reach new audiences—but they are likely to perceive your campaign within an extrinsic frame, and such campaigns are therefore less likely to promote a deeper concern about the natural world.[15]

This does not rule out the use of celebrities entirely: some are known for things other than money and status. Hugh Fearnley-Whittingstall, for instance, known to be passionate about ethical, locally-sourced food, is involved in the Fish Fight campaign. The values he embodies make him a good spokesperson on conservation issues.

Think through the effect your media stories and spokespeople are likely to have on people's values.

Try asking:
What values does the story embody? What three things first come to mind when you mention your celebrity spokesperson to someone? Do you associate these things with intrinsic or extrinsic values?

Try to:
Think about the emotional responses stories might generate, and how to highlight that issues are being addressed.

Focus on aspects of a story that highlight intrinsic values: community, concern for children and future generations, and the natural places that people care about.

Avoid economic framing and over-reliance on threat and fear.

Avoid picking a celebrity spokesperson based only on their perceived popularity.

Working with business

Engaging with the private sector is seen as important in order to achieve significant change. In doing so, it is important to also consider the values implications.

Corporate partnerships

Relationships with the private sector can take many forms—from event sponsorships to product tie-ins and 'stewardship'-type relationships. Conservation groups carefully weigh the environmental and financial costs and benefits of these relationships—but they could also consider the values they will promote.

Many businesses have a positive or neutral effect on society and the environment; some may have values much like those of the conservation sector. Others will have conflicting values, damaging the environment directly or promoting values (such as power and achievement) that impede environmental progress.

→ Recommendations

Carefully consider how a corporate partnership will affect people's values before proceeding with it.

Think about the kind of society your organisation is aiming for. Would this business be a part of it?

What do people associate with the business? What values might this evoke? Many companies that use 'green' branding will still promote extrinsic values and unsustainable consumption.

Avoid choosing a business partner only for the income you will gain or short-term environmental benefits you will achieve.

Cashing in on consumerism

Many conservation groups use commercial practices to raise money: some larger NGOs, for instance, offer a branded credit card. The case study below describes another scheme.

→ **Case study: The Give as you Live app**

The 'Give as you Live' app allows people to contribute to a charity of their choice when shopping: the app can be used at selected retailers, and a donation is made every time a purchase is made. While this can help raise money, it is likely to influence people's values, by:

- Endorsing consumerism indiscriminately. Many goods—such as patio heaters or flights—help destroy wildlife and disconnect us from the environment;
- Allowing users to feel they have 'done their bit' and need not do anything more. As the 'Give as you Live' website puts it: 'Just by shopping online, you can raise over £50 for your favourite charity—without putting your hand deeper into your pocket';
- Equating 'living' with shopping—when shopping is often associated with extrinsic values;
- Framing environmental groups as strongly associated with consumer products. The website displays a live feed showing what has been bought and how much has been donated, with the company's logo presented with the charity's logo. This could cause problems in the longer term, as environmental organisations may become associated with extrinsic values.

→ **Recommendation**

Carefully consider whether the money raised outweighs the risk of reinforcing extrinsic values.

Measuring success

Sometimes a campaign or project encourages people to act beyond its direct aims but in ways that are still in line with the wider aims of the organisation. Volunteering to plant trees, for instance, might encourage us to buy recycled paper afterwards, as we feel more concerned about forests. However, this can also work in the opposite direction: a campaign could unintentionally promote behaviours that are against the organisation's overall goal. These could at times outweigh the positive impacts of the campaign. Text informing people of the money-saving benefits of car share schemes, for instance, may make people less likely to recycle after reading the material.[16]

Membership figures, media presence and ecological trends do not measure conservation organisations' full impact.

New ways to measure success

Below, we suggest some better indicators of long-term success—many of which conservation groups already measure, and of which there will be many more:

○ Volunteer hours and volunteer enjoyment;
○ The ecological footprints of members before and after campaigns (see next section);
○ Noticeable shifts in government language (from extrinsic frames to intrinsic);
○ Number of people accessing green spaces after a campaign or activity.

Measures that the sector could look at together:

○ Outdoor activities in schools;
○ Access to green space;
○ Reduction in purchases of consumer goods;
○ Awareness and knowledge about species and the environment.

New measures for success in society

'This planet has—or rather had—a problem, which was this: most of the people living on it were unhappy for pretty much all of the time. Many solutions were suggested for this problem, but most of these were largely concerned with the movement of small green pieces of paper, which was odd because on the whole it wasn't the small green pieces of paper that were unhappy.' [17]

Douglas Adams

GDP, as a growing number of economists and academics have argued, is an inadequate measure of progress that fails to account for human and environmental wellbeing. This is important for conservation groups, as the narrow pursuit of economic growth at the expense of society and the environment may also erode the values that underpin social and environmental concern.

Alternative indicators, by contrast—such as the new economics foundation's National Accounts of Wellbeing—take social and environmental factors into consideration. Refocusing on these goals will likely reinforce intrinsic values.

→ **Recommendations**

Re-examine how you measure success with a consideration of values.

Think about what behaviours you want to encourage and try and measure these.

Consider working together as a sector to look at general trends around engagement with nature.

Support campaigns for an alternative to GDP as a measure of progress.

Measuring the effect you are having on values

Clearly organisations cannot stop appealing to extrinsic values altogether, but should be aware of the trade-offs.

Most projects will have a simple, easily-measured objective: a new policy or a certain number of new members, for instance. Broader impacts—including on values—are less obvious and harder to measure, and so tend to go unnoticed.

→ Example: Evaluating the impact on values

Many campaigns and projects set out with an easily measured objective in mind, such as government adoption of a policy, or a number of new members. Wider impacts—such as the impact on values—tend to go unnoticed, as they are less obvious and harder to measure.

The campaign

Suppose that an organisation is considering a campaign encouraging people to insulate their lofts. The campaign would focus on the cost-savings to householders of this one-off decision, using messages such as: 'By insulating your loft you could save yourself thousands of pounds!' The types of considerations the organisation should take into account are outlined in the table on the following page.

Making the trade-off

The intended aim of the campaign may be the most important consideration: loft insulation can have a major positive impact on people's overall greenhouse gas emissions.

In practice, however, the other impacts are likely to be significant, and may even outweigh these benefits. It may be tempting to ignore impacts that are difficult to measure, but if we are serious about our environmental goals they cannot be disregarded.

Potential impacts of the campaign	How could we measure this?
INTENDED OBJECTIVE OF THE CAMPAIGN: Increased uptake of loft insulation	No. of households participating.
CARBON IMPACTS: Effect on carbon footprints: a) Domestic energy demand may decline, or b) There may be rebound effects—participants simply enjoying warmer houses and consuming the same amount of energy.	Energy use before and after insulation.
VALUES IMPACT 1: The campaign may have the following impacts on other pro-environmental behaviour: a) 'Foot-in-the-door' effects: people may be encouraged to engage in other environmental behaviours (e.g. recycling); b) People may conclude that they have 'done their bit', reducing their motivation to engage in other pro environmental behaviours; c) It may strengthen the idea that people should only carry out environmental behaviours when they benefit too, or d) People may consider the campaign a money-saving exercise unconnected to the environment.	Studies of participants' overall environmental footprint.
VALUES IMPACT 2: Effects on a participant's willingness to take up wider pro-social behaviours. If the campaign is extrinsically-focused, these will be negative.	Observation of key behaviours; surveys.
VALUES IMPACT 3: Impacts on a wider, non-participating audience. Many thousands of people are likely to see the campaign material and not act on it. Extrinsic values will also impact them.	Measuring this impact is difficult, but such impacts should be considered.

→ Recommendation

Careful reflection like the one above should be carried out before campaigns, and the wider impacts measured where possible.

Values in working practices

An organisation is made up of its people—and people in nature conservation share many values. The structures and relationships within an organisation will either bolster or suppress the values, wellbeing and problem-solving capacity of its members.

Empowering people

Regardless of the size of an organisation, trusting people to make independent decisions and providing them space to explore ideas will enhance their motivation and overall effectiveness (promoting autonomy can reinforce intrinsic self-direction values).

Building trust and cohesion

Building understanding between colleagues can foster community and intrinsic values and mean people are more likely to act with concern for each other and the environment.

Bringing nature to work

Embed the experience and love of nature in your organisation and you will reinforce the intrinsic values of your staff.

Encourage autonomy and make room for creative collaboration.

'Hot-desking' for all staff (including managers) can increase links between different parts of an organisation and levels of seniority.

Shared, communal activities—shared lunches, or outings into green spaces—can also foster intrinsic values (but are unlikely to achieve enough on their own).

Find ways to allow staff to talk about what motivates them and about nature outside the narrow requirements of their job. The natural world is at the heart of your organisation, and keeping it there will connect you with the motivations of members and supporters. Begin each staff meeting by asking everyone present about the best wildlife or nature experience they had that week.

Create opportunities for all your staff to get out into nature; keep plants in the office; and encourage sustainable behaviours across the organisation. This will reinforce people's intrinsic motivations and focus on the environment.

Campaigning on Common Causes

To secure lasting public commitment to environmental protection, organisations should consider acting to strengthen society's intrinsic values and weaken extrinsic values.

Our society is not a blank slate; there are many things that are currently acting to influence people's behaviour. Consider the policies, institutions and experiences that shape society's values—they may offer major campaigning opportunities. Small interventions in these areas can have a big impact, because of the values they strengthen (and weaken).

We offer a few examples below.

Time and income poverty

People in the UK are overworked, with limited leisure time. With poverty on the rise, the desire for economic security will cause many to focus on extrinsic values; while a lack of time and money will prevent them from visiting green spaces.

Campaign suggestions

Campaign to increase minimum paid holiday; campaign for employees to have the option of a four-day working week; campaign for increased public transport provision.

Advertising and consumerism

We are constantly marketed at; told we need to buy increasing amounts. This is environmentally destructive and reinforces extrinsic values at the same time.

Campaign suggestions

Campaign for a ban on intrusive outdoor advertising; campaign for a ban on advertising to children; campaign to ban environmentally-damaging products being advertised using natural scenes.

→ **Example: Leave Our Kids Alone**

Recently-launched campaign Leave Our Kids Alone aims to ban advertising to children aged 11 and under, noting that similar laws are in force in Quebec, Norway, Sweden and Greece. While many other regulations protect children's physical and mental wellbeing, the campaign points out no such restrictions affect advertising—even where it is consciously designed to exploit and manipulate.

Leave Our Kids Alone would benefit from the support of organisations across the third sector, and will likely help address some of the roots of extrinsic values.

Media bias

There is a strong bias towards negative messages and economics in the media. This increases feelings of insecurity and extrinsic values.

Campaign suggestion

Campaign against the prominence of economic coverage on BBC news; or for the level of CO_2 in the atmosphere to get the same level of attention as the FTSE 100.

As far outside of the remit of conservation as these issues seem to be, issues like this should be addressed in order to increase long-term active support for issues core to conservation.

Working together for a strong sector

It is unrealistic to suggest that large-scale change can come from organisations working on their own. Organisations can work together more, connected by the values they want to strengthen.

The third sector risks undermining its own efforts by strengthening extrinsic values. Some strategies might undermine successes—such as raising more money. By eroding public concern and action, the work of the conservation sector is eroded overall. By reinforcing each other's efforts, each organisation can make the sector stronger.

Challenging extrinsic frames and reconnecting people with nature will require a concerted effort. Any group challenging the economic valuation of wildlife on its own, for instance, will lack the force of a cross-sector coalition.

Understanding how intrinsic values link social and environmental concern can open up the potential for unlikely alliances—much as the Wild Network[18] includes organisations concerned with health, child wellbeing, conservation, and others. Conservation organisations are not unfamiliar with working together—whether through the collective voice of Wildlife and Countryside Link or broad coalitions such as Stop Climate Chaos. Existing links like this could be used to work together.

There are also new collaborative styles, like the Collective Impact model outlined by the Stanford Social Innovation Review (see the following page), and other methods specifically designed for complex issues. Organisations could explore these models further.

→ **Recommendations**

Explore new ways of working together.

Try not to undermine the work of others by appealing to extrinsic values or using other frames that are unhelpful to conservation or to encouraging action.

Strengthen relationships between organisations, through secondments between NGOs, or days volunteering for others.

→ **Collective Impact: ways of working well together**

The Collective Impact model was outlined by the Stanford Social Innovation Review.[19]

Common Agenda: All partners should have a common understanding of the problem and a shared vision of the solution.

Shared Measurement Systems are essential if you want to make an impact.

Mutually Reinforcing Activities: Collaborative projects involve a variety of roles: they do not require everyone to do the same thing.

Continuous Communication: Regular meetings and feedback are essential.

Backbone Support Organisations: A separate organisation with specific skills should act as manager, serving as a backbone for the entire coalition.

These principles enable staff to learn as they go and react to problems and opportunities as they emerge, in a manner consistent with the common agenda, while the backbone organisation facilitates this process. When properly set in motion, this process helps coalitions act effectively under constantly changing circumstances.

What areas of your organisation's work do you think have the biggest impact on values?

For which other areas of work does this have implications?

What specific policy changes do you think will achieve what is necessary?

Which policy areas that affect values could your organisation work on?

Conclusion
Values: a crossroads for conservation

"**Another world is not only possible,
she is on her way. On a quiet day,
I can hear her breathing.**"

Arundhati Roy

Values: a crossroads for conservation

To create and maintain a wildlife-rich, sustainable society, we need concerned, connected and active citizens. Working together, there is a chance to make this a reality.

Achieving the goals of conservation requires a public that demands change, and a political system capable of rising to this challenge.

An understanding of values sheds light on how communications and experiences can nurture a person's sense of connectedness to the natural world and motivate them to act. This understanding also highlights the countless conservation activities (too many to do justice to in this guide!) that are already doing just that, as well as new opportunities for creating change.

Fostering values such as self-acceptance, care for others, and concern for the natural world can have real and lasting benefits in conservation. By using this understanding to identify new areas for policies and campaigning, and by working together to cultivate these intrinsic values, we can create a society that is more compassionate, more connected to nature, and more motivated to protect our environment for generations to come.

Why does conservation matter to you?

What would you like to see change in nature conservation?

Further reading for the keen and sceptical...

The full report, *Common Cause for Nature*, outlines more on the evidence base behind the values approach, and the full research methodology and results of the communications analysis.

If you're interested in reading even more about Common Cause and the values approach, read:

The Common Cause Handbook
Tim Holmes, Elena Blackmore, Richard Hawkins and Tom Wakeford, (2011).

Common Cause: the case for working with our cultural values
Tom Crompton, (2010).

Both can be found at
valuesandframes.org/downloads

If you'd like to read about children's disconnection from the outdoors, read:

Natural Childhood
Stephen Moss, (2012).

Free Range Kids
Sustrans, (2011).

For an exploration of the cultural impact of advertising, see:

Think of Me as Evil? Opening the ethical debates in advertising
Jon Alexander, Tom Crompton and Guy Shrubsole, (2012).

To read more about motivation at work, read:

Drive: the surprising truth about what motivates us
Dan Pink, (2009).

The Nature of Nature Conservationists: an investigation into value, motivation and ontology within the field of nature conservation
Cara Roberts, (2010).

*The Nature of Nature Conservationists: How well do organisational
and individual aspirations match?*
Gabrielle Horup, (2010).

Case studies and examples mentioned:

DEFRA
gov.uk/government/policies/protecting-biodiversity-and-ecosystems-
at-home-and-abroad

Stalled Spaces
glasgow.gov.uk/stalledspaces

Greenpeace Compass
greenpeacecompass.org/gpc/Common/Page/MissionStatement

National Accounts of Wellbeing
nationalaccountsofwellbeing.org

Leave Our Kids Alone
leaveourkidsalone.org

Collective Impact
ssireview.org/articles/entry/collective_impact

"Everything in nature invites us constantly to be what we are."

Gretel Ehrlich

References

1 GlobeScan (2013). *Environmental Concern 2013*. Available at: http://www.globescan.com/images/images/pressreleases/ 2013-Enviro-Radar/globescan_press_release_enviroconcern_03-25-2013.pdf (Accessed April 19, 2013).

2 Sheldon, K. M. & Kasser, T. (2008). *Psychological Threat and Extrinsic Goal Striving. Motivation and Emotion* 32(1): 37-45.; Harr, B. N. (2012). *Psychology for a Better World*. University of Auckland.

3 Schwartz, S. H. (1992). *Universals in the Content and Structure of Values: Theoretical Advances and Empirical Tests in 20 Countries*. In M. Zanna (Ed.), *Advances in Experimental Social Psychology Vol. 25* (pages 1–65). New York: Academic Press; Schwartz, S. H., Cieciuch, J., Vecchione, M., Davidov, E., Fischer, R., Beierlein, C., Ramos, A., Verkasalo, M., Lönnqvist, J.-E., Demirutku, K., Dirilen-Gumus, O. & Konty, M. (2012). Refining the theory of basic individual values. *Journal of Personality and Social Psychology*, 103(4), 663–88. This research is discussed in more detail in *Common Cause for Nature: understanding values and frames in the conservation sector*.

4 Maio, G. R., Pakizeh, A., Cheung, W.-Y. & Rees, K. J. (2009). Changing, priming, and acting on values: effects via motivational relations in a circular model. *Journal of Personality and Social Psychology*, 97(4), 699–715. *Common Cause* also outlines many more examples (see *Further reading for the keen and sceptical...* at the end of this guide).

5 Chilton, P., Crompton, T., Kasser, T., Maio, G. & Nolan, A. (2012). *Communicating bigger-than-self problems to extrinsically-oriented audiences*. Common Cause (pages 1–52). Available at: http://valuesandframes.org/downloads/ (Accessed on April 22, 2013). There are many other studies that show similar effects.

6 Schwartz, S. H. & Bardi, A. (2001). Value hierarchies across cultures: taking a similarities perspective. *Journal of Cross-Cultural Psychology*, 32(3), 268–290.

7 Bauer, M. A., Wilkie, J. E., Kim, J. K. & Bodenhausen, G. V. (2012). Cuing consumerism: situational materialism undermines personal and social well-being. *Psychological Science*, 23(5), 517–523.

8 Taken from: http://www.redtapechallenge.cabinetoffice.gov.uk/home/index/ (Accessed April 19, 2013).

9 Rudd, M., Vohs, K. D. & Aaker, J. (2012). Awe expands people's perception of time, alters decision making, and enhances well-being. *Psychological Science*, 23(10), 1130-1136.

10 Horup, G. (2010). *The Nature of Nature Conservationists: how well do organisational and individual aspirations match?* Unpublished dissertation, Birbeck College, the University of London.

11 Serra-Barragán, L. (2012). *A Psychological Games Approach to Motivation Crowding-out: The Case of Payments for Environmental Services*. Unpublished paper; the University of Warwick. Available at: http://www2.warwick.ac.uk/fac/ soc/economics/staff/phd_students/serra_barragan/luis_serra_job_market_paper.pdf (Accessed April 22, 2013).

12 Thøgersen, J. & Crompton, T. (2009). Simple and painless? The limitations of spillover in environmental campaigning. *Journal of Consumer Policy*, 32(2), 141–163.

13 Baker, N. quoted in: Moss, S. (2012). *Natural Childhood*. The National Trust, (page 17). Available at: http://www. heritageinschools.ie/fileadmin/user_upload/documents/Research_reports/National-Trust-natural_childhood.pdf (Accessed April 22, 2013).

14 Interviewee for *Common Cause for Nature*, written communication, (2013).

15 O'Neill, S. J., Boykoff, M., Niemeyer, S. & Day, S. A. (2013). On the use of imagery for climate change engagement. *Global Environmental Change*.

16 Evans, L., Maio, G. R., Corner, A., Hodgetts, C. J., Ahmed, S. & Hahn, U. (2012). *Self-interest and pro-environmental behaviour. Nature Climate Change*, 2(8), 1–4.

17 Adams, D. (1980). *The Hitch-Hiker's Guide to the Galaxy*. London: Pan Macmillan.

18 The partnership that formed following the *Natural Childhood* report.

19 Kania, J. & Kramer, M. (2011). *Collective Impact*. Available at: http://www.ssireview.org/articles/entry/collective_impact (Accessed on 10 May, 2013).

Photo credits

Cover:
Matt Adam Williams

Pages 4 & 5:
Matt Adam Williams

Pages 16 & 17:
Tom Mason (c)

Pages 18 & 19:
Tom Mason (c)

Pages 30 & 31:
Adelph Studio (c)

Pages 32 & 33:
Jane Corey (c), Silent Valley Gwent Wildlife Trust Nature Reserve

Pages 46 & 47:
Matt Adam Williams

Pages 52 & 53:
Richard Fisher

Pages 74 & 75:
Jacki Clark (c), John Muir Award

Pages 100 & 101:
Matt Adam Williams

Pages 104 & 105:
Haydn West (c), Bat Conservation Trust: Bat Children

Pages 108 & 109:
Katrina Martin

By printing this publication on Cocoon Offset 100% recycled paper, the environmental impact was reduced by:

- 1,059 kg of landfill
- 20,726 litres of water
- 1,951 kWh of electricity
- 198 kg CO_2 and greenhouse gases
- 1,720 kg of wood

Source: Carbon footprint data evaluated by FactorX in accordance with the Bilan Carbone® methodology. Calculations are based on a comparison between the recycled paper used versus a virgin fibre paper according to the latest European BREF data (virgin fibre paper) available.

Results are obtained according to techinical information and are subject to modification.

ARJOWIGGINS
G R A P H I C

Printed on Cocoon Offset 300gsm cover and 120gsm text, made from 100% recycled fibre, certified FSC® recycled.